Dedication

To my three children (Waylon, DeWayne and Kyleigh) may you always know how much you are loved!

I love you most in all the Milky Way
~Mommy

Published by
GRAPH Publishing, L.L.C.
www.graphpublishing.com

Printed in the U.S.A.

I love you most in all the Milky Way

By Shelby McKelvain

GRAPH
Publishing, L.L.C.

About The Author

Shelby McKelvain is a Christian woman who seeks to live each day with faith at the center of her heart and home. She believes that marriage, motherhood, and daily acts of service are sacred callings, and she strives to honor God by placing Him first in all she does. Her life is shaped by prayer, gratitude, and a desire to cultivate a home filled with peace, purpose, and love.

Shelby graduated from Hardin-Simmons University in 2016 with a Bachelor of Fine Arts. Soon after, God led her to marry her husband, Brandon, the love of her life and a constant source of strength and support. Together they are raising their three children—Waylon, DeWayne, and Kyleigh—whom Shelby considers her greatest earthly blessings. She embraces motherhood as a ministry, guiding her children not only in their education, but in their faith, character, and understanding of God's truth.

As a stay-at-home mother, Shelby homeschools her children, viewing each lesson and each day as an opportunity to plant seeds of wisdom, curiosity, and spiritual growth. Alongside her role at home, she also helps run a book publishing company, Graph Publishing, L.L.C., where she supports creative work that encourages, uplifts, and inspires others.

Shelby finds deep joy in the rhythms of homemaking. She loves tending a garden, creating with her hands, spending time outdoors, and cooking and baking from scratch—simple practices she sees as acts of stewardship and gratitude. She continually seeks to learn new homemaking skills, believing that caring for her home and family is a meaningful way to serve God and those He has entrusted to her.

Above all, Shelby's life is a testimony to her desire to walk faithfully with God, trusting Him in every season and finding beauty in a life lived with intention, humility, and love.

Shelby created this book as a bedtime story to remind her children—always—how deeply they are loved. "I love you most in all the Milky Way" is a special saying and game they share. She will say, "I love you most in all the Milky Way," and they'll answer with something even bigger, like, "I love you most in all the galaxy" or "the universe" or "in all of God's creation"

Never stop teaching your children about God, and never stop telling them how much you love them—no matter how old they may be.

Look up boys, and count as many stars as you can see in the heavens above.

One, two, three, four, five...
Mommy we can't count all the stars
there are too many.

Yes, my babies, it is impossible for us to count all the stars in the night sky.

God determines the number of the stars. Great is our Lord and mighty in power. He brings out the starry host one by one as He calls them by name. Because of his great power and mighty strength, not one star is missing.

Now my loves crawl into bed and look out the window at the twinkling stars. Know that God's blanket of stars in the night sky will cover the darkness with light.

Let us bow our heads and say our prayers.

Dear God, thank you for the stars that light the night, thank you for our family and our many blessings. Forgive me of my wrongs I made today. Guide us and protect us. Amen

Goodnight my babies, sleep tight and know that Mommy loves you most in all the Milky Way.

The boys whispered back "Mommy we love you most in all the universe."

"But, I love you most in all of God's creation, now to sleep with you both." she loveling whispered back.

Psalms 147:4-5
"He determines the number of the stars and calls them each by name. Great is our Lord and mighty in power; his understanding has no limit."

Isaiah 40:26
"Lift up your eyes and look to the heavens: Who created all these? He who brings out the starry host one by one and calls forth each of them by name. Because of his great power and mighty strength, not one of them is missing."

Prayers

This story includes simple prayers to guide children as they pray each day and night. It softly leads little hearts to give thanks, ask for forgiveness, and speak to God with trust, gratitude, and love. These prayers remind children that God is always listening, and that through prayer they can find comfort, peace, and protection, resting safely in His constant presence.

The Lord's Prayer

Our Father, who art in heaven,
hallowed be thy name,
thy kingdom come, thy will be one,
on Earth as it is in heaven.

Give us this day our daily bread.
And forgive us our trespasses,
as we forgive those who trespass against
us. And lead us not into temptation,
but deliver us from evil.

Amen.

Gratitude Prayer

Thank you, Lord, for loving me,
Thank you for my family.
Thank you for the sunny days.
Thank you for guiding all of my ways.

Thank you for teaching me
about your love.
Thank you for coming
down from above.
To make a way to know You more.
Thank you, Jesus. Thank you, Lord.

Amen.

Guidance Prayer

Oh Lord,
give me eyes to see,
ears to hear,
minds to understand,
hearts to believe, and
mouths to tell others
of Your love and salvation.

Amen.

Bedtime Prayer

Now I lay me down to sleep,
I pray the Lord my soul to keep,
May God guard me through the night,
And wake me with the morning light.

Amen.

Daily Prayer

Thank you, Lord, for this day.
Lead my steps and light my way.
May what I do please You today.
In Your powerful name, I pray.

Amen.

www.ingramcontent.com/pod-product-compliance
Lightning Source LLC
Chambersburg PA
CBHW041612120626
46551CB00002B/414